United States distributor
DUFOUR EDITIONS, INC.
Booksellers and Publishers
Chester Springs, Pennsylvania 19425

ROY FULLER

From the Joke Shop

 ANDRE DEUTSCH

TO ANTHONY AND VIOLET POWELL

First published 1975 by
André Deutsch Limited
105 Great Russell Street London WC1

Printed in Great Britain by
Clarke, Doble and Brendon Ltd
Plymouth

1SBN 0 233 96670 6

AUTHOR'S NOTE

I read somewhere (after writing poem XVII) that Goethe disliked dogs, so it seems unlikely that he owned one. The book the title of which is the title of poem LVII is by Phillips and Bazett and printed by C.W. Poole and Sons of Chelmsford. The book referred to in poem XII is Peter Brown's *The World of Late Antiquity* (Thames and Hudson): borrowings from it appear in several other poems. The composer of the film music referred to in poem LV may merely be unknown to me.

CONTENTS

I BEFORE

A drift of feathers in my way across
The park made by a rational century
Returns me to the plains of Africa.

The corpse not there, the crime unspeakable —
This is the nature reason mitigates
And yet is helpless when confronted by.

I think about the dying bird brought in —
The neighbour seizing on our catlessness.
By a coincidence, not rare in man's

Affairs, it proved to be the orphaned stare
I'd stood as sentinel and victualler for.
Perhaps some lack in me had then compelled

Its anabasis to another lawn
Where it did battle with a feline foe.
Hope sparked at first, though swiftly doom came down.

I put the bird upon the grass to die
But when it spun on frantic, feeble wings
I snatched it up and held it at my throat.

I might have had it there still (I suppose)
If warmth and anguish could have kept it quick.
Alas, with grace it bowed *its* throat for ever.

I wonder if I smoothed that voyage all
Must take. Or not. Undoubtedly its neck
Was always arched too far. As youthful necks

So nearly are, without the stroke of death.

II KANTIAN MATTERS

I.m. Kenneth Allott 1912-73

The years arrive and go and are forgotten

The tone inevitably elegiac:
As Gilbert Murray said, one cannot write
'And after many a summer dies the duck.'

Drinking the wines of '70 — absurd.
Poet a century hence, to whom your fellow
Bards have been known to appeal, you're almost here!

And we ourselves have doddered on to odd
Times and must try for urban philistines
To make sense out of prosody and dawns.

Yet my contemporaries are dying round me.
Even those silent since their youth seem gagged
Just as their lips were forming some great message.

And more persistent singers by that token
Look to have cheated death, despite our having
To watch them shrink and whiten in their clothes.

After the bird expired between my palms
And I had buried it, I thought: 'You missed
The fireball at nine. And all the ruffling rain.'

Who knows which cataclysm is the worst,
Nature's or history's? I see today
Fasces protruding from a lion's jaw —

Thoughtless baroque idea of decorating
The purlieus of learning and high oratory.
It only means brute's triumph over brute.

The State sicks up the violent element
That breeds in its craw. 'The old age of certain men
Is like the childhood of immortality.'

— Thus the Goncourts. What change has come to life
In a hundred years! How unserene my soul!
Yet the two Kantian matters still remain

For admiration: first, the moral law
Within us; secondly, the stellar sky
Above us — outside our rooms, our self-regard,

That haunt our years and flick them swiftly through.

III   CONSOLATIONS OF ART

For Jack Lindsay

J.M.W. Turner on Switzerland:
'The Country on the whole surpasses Wales.'
— As parsimonious with praise as cash.

It was this little down-to-brass-tacks man
Who saw that nature, history and time
Were mostly fields for Cataclysm's advent;

And on his 'waking eye' (he wrote in verse)
'Rushed the still ruins of dejected Rome.'
The exciting revolution also brings

A constant sense of parallel disasters —
As well I know, who followed '17
Like artists who came after '89.

No doubt the dying age, not dying fast;
The new society murdered in its youth;
The need for stoic individuals

Recall the line of empty cities, force
Poets to see in all phenomena
(Even in landscape) culture's coming doom.

A sky of Turner's, said the critics, is
'A heap of marble mountains.'
The painter himself observed about a salad

(Conversing with his neighbour at a dinner):
'A nice cool green that lettuce, isn't it?
The beetroot pretty red though not quite strong enough.

Add mustard and you've got an oil of mine!'
Despairing of the State, Euripides
Became a quietist. Thus creators end.

IV   INSOMNIA

A memory of some preposterous
Experience makes me realise that at last
I must have dozed; and getting up to shut

The window on an aircraft's whinny, note
The curtain's crack still sabled by the night.
What cries and danger do I also damp?

And all in vain, since worse are in my head.
At eighty-five Stravinsky saw his birth
Certificate ('very yellow') in a dream.

I start myself towards historic age,
Shocked by obituaries of contemporaries,
Thinking that I'm becoming odd enough

Myself to tempt a spare biographer;
The habit of friendship, as of life itself,
Turned to a whim of waking up or not.

Then, after more of Robert Craft, cold drinks,
Hot drinks and pees have somehow doodled in
The cipher hours of insomnia,

I see from my study, in the morning sun,
That what were formerly judged a dirty brown —
Cock sparrows' periwigs — are really auburn.

To understand the brute: not difficult
In view of all the sensitivity
Engendered by the night. More speculative:

Having to live with humankind. That bird
Only when dying would allow itself
To be embraced. Quite other with most men —

Demanding to be loved for qualities
Unlovable . . . And so the pen runs on,
Trying to bring together what it knows

To be least trivial: not rhetoric, facts;
And failing. For in art I'm timid as
In life. The summer burns the best away;

Umbrellas flying to the fists of clerks,
Leaving the operating-table bare —
At least, save for the suffering aptly there.

V   DEAD POET

Going across the piebald summer green,
By the glass pond, the willow's waterfall,
I wonder suddenly if I shall see you

In one of your familiar emanations —
With walking-stick, perhaps, or musing on
A bench of the municipality.

At once I remember you are dead. A step
More on the slippery beige and then the thought:
But shan't we soon be meeting, after all?

Fanciful concept, since I disbelieve
In after-life. Nor shall I join you in
Some notional pantheon of immortal bards —

11

Part of the irony of coming death
Is just its confirmation one's to be,
Despite a life of trying otherwise,

A nonentity. No doubt too late I note
That people usually choose as favourites,
Out of my poems, pieces (all too few)

On the demise of cats, or filial guilt.
It seems I rarely found the common touch,
Though my emotions common as they come.

Drawn to a tapping stick run creviced ants,
More than a hundred times as old as man.
The heart being recently invented, they

Own just a cardiac vessel. Poets sunk
Within their art ostensibly possess
Such myrmecoid heartlessness in life itself,

Yet, as one's circle, like a dish of cherries,
Gradually decreases to the tough
Or the deformed, how copious the tears!

The chairs stay out all night. Shall I get through
The shortening days to laze in them again,
And say once more: I'll savour these at least —

Make go as slowly as the gnomon's shade,
Or even stop, like green nasturtium wheels;
Spending more time out in the hedgehog's moon?

August itself has undertones of Fall,
Some inexplicable, imperial,
Elgarian sadness. Don't we long to assume,

As simply as the starling, winter plumage,
See off our final brood in mellow days,
Die stoically, and carefully out of sight?

Licking each other and exchanging food —
Is how ants spend their lives. So far as men
Swerve from that model is the measure of

Unhappiness, what makes precisely for
The human: culture of neurosis — cities
Ant-riddled from scratch, chronicled by the sky.

VI   CHANCE

At lunch I mention one who was a child —
Of brains — I knew twelve years ago. That night
I dream I take the hand of such a child.

Profound beyond her years, she then remarks
My tender interest is erotic; and
Indeed I see her breast is slightly curved.

I say I'll keep that element remote;
And really that is what I would prefer.
She smiles. Is not convinced. Then I awake.

The reason I let fall the name was that
I'd seen her husband lunching in the place,
With a blonde girl I thought at first the wife.

No dark affair was thrown up by this chance
So far as I'm aware — no more than life's
Normal coincidence and consequence.

Though, as I write that, I'm appalled at what
May possibly ensue. So I cut short
My workings-out, both real and in the mind

In case they can be used to alter fate
Or that my phantasies may hurt too much
A fair girl's selfless care for deepest themes . . .

I glimpsed a flourished hand splash out some wine.
How different from my own bibacious rites!
Life, in a dozen years, transformed to dreams.

VII   IN PRAISE OF WAKEFULNESS

Theatre light draws me out upon the lawn.
The middle of the night: two garden-chairs
Under the yellow moon and Jupiter.

Both empty: somehow I expected them
(Or one, more likely) to be occupied.
It is as though we'd left the house for good —

That curious epoch, sometimes talked about,
When others' furniture is in our rooms
And strange flowers in the new-shaped borders blow.

I read Craft on Stravinsky, back in bed.
In retrospect it's just those moments when
He's pissed that make his life for him worth while.

One must enjoy the migraine blur of moons
In the binoculars' image of the orb,
Unsatisfactory as it is; enjoy

The prospect of recovery in that chair,
In sunlight, from a night of sleeplessness;
And, more than that, enjoy the actual,

The bothersome nights themselves, which after all
Are ludicrously shorter than the night
Through which one's sleep will be without a flaw.

After my death may well turn up that file
Recording jests for use when speechifying.
What extra wry banality revealed!

How, Beachcomber enquired, to cure a red
Nose? Answer: go on drinking till it turns
Purple. Here's to insomnia, the worse the better!

VIII   VARIATIONS

For John Lehmann

According to a *TLS* review
Franck 'led an uneventful life . . . was not . . .
Prolific'. Might have been describing me.

The window frames a leggy yellow rose.
I hurry out to rescue drowning bees.
The bedside notebook yields its gibberish.

Franck: many boring bars; a schmaltzy tune;
Arguably, wit and singularity
Confined to the *Variations symphoniques*.

Not bad to be remembered even thus.
Each decade trendy geniuses arise;
Non-geniuses nearer to oblivion.

Ancients on benches, crumbling bread for birds —
It's they I should be with! Don't mind the young
Doing what's daring: I just want to think it.

The games of human love are infantile,
Admittedly: my tragi-comedy
Is seeing them as puerile as well.

Making the relative allowances,
You're not, dear friend, as antique as your dog.
I can't yet pity you for walking slow

Or coughing when you rise to welcome me.
As for your fifty years' affair with iambs,
I envy it. No cause for faithlessness.

Creation seems continuous, looking back;
Yet we both know how random and how frail
The hours that make the opus numbers up.

I wish your study windows *cloches* for flowers . . .
More and more sweetness in your neighbours' hives . . .
Dreaming recalled and always metrical!

IX   READING IN THE NIGHT

In the Stravinsky book by Lillian Libman:
The old idea that this very hour
(Because the sun lies farthest off from man)

Is the worst hour of the twenty-four.
Initially surprised we still depend
On that outmoded god, that dying fire,

One soon is reconciled — for, after all,
The star had grandeur and is ours alone.
Besides, far back it gave us life, although

We now may look askance at the donation.
The ambiguities of day return.
Light enough to discover with a pang

A spider drowned, like scribble, in a bucket.
Yet seeing that emblematic, as if art
Had vanquished superstition, even death;

As if one didn't know the final plight —
For it to be beyond our human powers
Even to orchestrate another's fugue.

X   ORPHANS

Product of pigeon love — pale legs and beak,
Dark plumage ruffled in a boyish way,
Behaviour vulnerable and innocent.

16

Who would have thought the conscientiousness
Events built into me in youth would be
One day directed to concern about

A fledgling pigeon extant suddenly
In the once carefree garden; parentless,
It seems, unwanted (least of all by me);

And helpless, more or less; and probably
A hopeless case? It's in my character
To feed, and guard it from the cats all day . . .

Wake to a dawn of worry . . . till at last,
Searching the spider-scuttling shrubbery's depths,
I have to admit the coming of its fate.

Strange that my poetry isn't taken up
(I mean by an audience more numerous)
Since cosiness seems my overwhelming wish.

Perhaps what jars — the echoes of remorse.
If I had only persevered I might
Have caged the fledgling safe from wandering.

Practice has let me almost overcome
The fear and repugnance that my fingers feel
For fluttering, and another's alien softness;

But what deterred me here I know of old —
A sense of not presuming to impose
My will, existence, ineffectual love.

Flaws of the mould on every replica
Made by a life — and to repeat itself
Is how life comes to be, alas, designed.

Calamitous, a bird's abandonment:
But what about my own young orphancy?
The unreachable corner where I hid or died?

Today it spends its life against a wall:
Facilities inside quite unemployed.
Its top can be unfolded and a leg

Swung round to make a battlefield of baize
With shallow cups to hold one's cash or chips
And zinc-based corner circlets for the drinks.

It comes down from my father and my youth.
Round it sat Issy Gotcliffe and the Weinbergs,
Powers in the textile trade in Manchester.

There I first stole an aromatic sip
Of scotch, midst laughs at my precocity:
Could be the last year of the First World War.

World vanished, almost in the mind as well —
Too young, my brother, to remember it.
All, save we supernumeraries, dead.

What point or virtue in remembering it?
Except to make it stand for everyone's
Possession of such a world — and of their loss.

The bearded faces carved upon the table's
Thighs (so to speak) will quite soon start to mean
Part of his childhood to another child.

His father will have had the enterprise
To lay out cash for art — extravagance
Condoned by delight and use, as ought to be.

My album of those days reveals that Issy
Served in the infantry — maybe in fact
He perished there, for all is speculative

In my recall, I'm sure; as history is.
At any rate, perhaps he never knew
How fascists tried to exterminate his kind.

Even in '18 he of course looked back
To times astoundingly myself had glimpsed —
A general peace, long days, illusive art.

'*Komm in den kleinen Pavillon,*' they sang —
Of *décor* amateurs would now reject:
Their heroes walrused; stout *grisettes*; and gay

Ill-fitting uniforms, to be exchanged
In a few years for real ones of field-grey.
Ah, music, not made cynical by Weill;

Love innocent in art and so in life;
Empires not cruel save through carelessness;
Summers of mere manoeuvres, courts of cards!

XII   LUDICROUS REFLECTIONS

Sunning myself (high summer in the garden),
My fingers brush against my solid thigh.
I think: quite good material for compost.

The unity of all organic stuff —
Some rationale behind that simple notion,
Although precisely what is hard to say.

If life were atomized, I mean, no chance
Of pre-lapsarian, spontaneous
Regeneration in the ensuing sludge.

In any case, what ludicrous reflections!
Even a friendly critic would pronounce
Such lines self-parody. Still more to come!

I raise my book and read that 'in the age
Of the Antonines we meet a surprising number
Of florid valetudinarians'.

No need to travel so far back in time,
No need to go to Rome to find the type
That takes the empire's sickness for his own.

I don't recall the gay, rich days — though born
In '12, my earliest memories include
Wondering what the Press would do in peace.

Maybe the sorrows of my infancy
Somehow foretold the sorrows of the times.
Even the sibling who survived with me

Was born the very day of deaths by sea
And claims of so-called victory off Jutland
By admirals on either archaic side.

Do bees go home? It's half-past six and yet
They water, still as cattle, at the bowl
Provided specially for such as they;

But where they sometimes drown or, frantic, must
Be rescued by a great and godlike index:
As we ourselves in this ambiguous world.

XIII   SHAKESPEARE AND CO

> *'Tis strange that death should sing* — King John

Late Beethoven quartets: Stravinsky, old,
Murmuring 'Wonderful! Incredible!'
— Which leads the memoirist to name a third

'Who might have joined them', he who 'out of some
Terrible suffering' wrote *Macbeth* and *Lear*,
Then in his final years emerged to give

'Supreme expression' of the sense of life,
To wit *The Tempest* and *The Winter's Tale*.
One's touched, in the context, by this corny view,

Though sure that suffering's what we all can share
With genius and it needn't be top-notch.
The Victorian painter, Richard Dadd, who stabbed,

He said, 'an individual who called
Himself my father', made for forty years
In Broadmoor wonderful, incredible fairy worlds.

The difference is the hand's resource and craft
That turn the cloudy visions of the mind
Into a change of key, a pacifist isle.

Still, strange enough that autumn period:
The fruit so easily could be detached
But nature through its thread hangs on to add

Colour to seeds, a variegated cheek,
Flesh ready for consuming. Chaos persists —
The troublesome reign, false friends' conspiracies —

Though far from the ailments and obituaries
That almost daily plague old age, but yet
Can't spoil (that, rather, must enhance) the sense

Only possessed by age — that, when all's said
And done, life isn't death, however frail
The finger following the heavenly score.

XIV   ELEPHANTS, ANTS, DOVES

801 — an elephant in Gaul!
They speak about the stagnant Middle Ages,
Of Islam cutting off the Middle Sea,

And yet the monster enterprisingly
Shuffled from Indian jungle to the Rhône.
Puzzling to tell one's place in history.

What lies before us now — a 'dark age' or
An all too necessary rebirth? A worse
Election looms because of man's new power

To liquidate not merely heretics
And enemies of state but life itself:
Life only geared to nature's cataclysms —

These ants that put their winged friends on their feet,
Like aircraft handlers, and those pigeons which,
From mutual nibbling at the exiguous face

And thrusting a bill far down the other's throat,
Take their respective postures in a sketchy
Rehearsal for prolonging pigeon life.

Social and private failure and success —
How like the human! But without its guilt
And its articulate recrimination.

Yes, I would sacrifice mankind if that
Could save the six-legged and the avian.
Though who's to say the formic city less

Unjust than ours, and that the dove, evolved,
Wouldn't impose tyrannical modes of love?
Let's pension off the soldiers, see what comes.

XV   FAMILY MATTERS

I. m. John Broadbent: ob. 3. ix. 1973

One of my mother's younger brothers dies:
My mother dead, my own age sixty-one.
The news originates in my native north.

Widowered, living in a small hotel,
He failed to wake today. He might have thought,
Going to bed, to amend some work of art —

Too late. Though I believe he'd not kept up
His talent as a water-colourist —
Making his mark as spare-time Thespian.

A mile from here one might, if one so wished,
Into the urban Thames expectorate.
It strikes me that I'm very far from home;

Yet this is where I've lived most of my life.
A sorrowing infant on the Pennine moors,
The borderer became a natural exile.

Or is it class that makes me sceptical:
Descendant of bloody-minded NCOs,
And probably reluctant patriots

Even in the Wars of the Roses? Yet from you —
Ironic, emotion-hiding distaff side —
Comes the true joy of life, creativeness.

Mysterious paternal ancestors,
I have to put you second in my life
To those who must have engineered my soul —

Soloists in *Elijah,* councillors
In local government, heroes of the sub-plot,
Parodists and analysts of tragic life.

How dark the trees grow when, the sun gone down,
I sit on in the young September's dusk
Until invisible against the west

The tiny flies, until a late bird soars
Too swiftly past to be identified,
Until the owl's repeated painful creak

Replaces all day's noises, and I can't
Quite see to write. One only has to choose
A different milieu for one's garden chair

Or just stay till an unfamiliar hour,
And life seems changed somehow — 'prolonged' would be
The word had not the thought come to me now

That last night, too, my uncle might have seen
Clouds first illumined by an orange light
Then disappear, the sky turn oyster grey;

The acacia leaves suspend themselves in black
And graduated brushstrokes either side
Of stems so slender as to be invisible.

XVI   DREAMS SACRED AND PROFANE

Our petrified existence with the dead
Haunts wakeful nights like cocktail memories
Sour with the senseless things we did or said.

'What is the *Lear*,' wrote Coleridge, 'the *Othello*
But a divine dream?' — thinking poetry
To be a dream the dreamer rationalized.
.

But to the author it's no thing of art,
The dream in which he always plays a part:
Merely a run of boobs he can't expunge.

Why should he make the dead come back in dreams;
And re-enact their hurt and his neglect?
Slumbering or not, unsatisfactory nights!

Between the boiler-house and garden-shed
September mornings trail a filament
Across my brow: this year a prelude to

Uncanny subsequence of cloudless dusks —
No more to do with troubled early hours
Than evolution's ingenuity

With man's quite likely self-willed holocaust.
Indeed, perhaps life's something up its sleeve:
Seeds of the arctic lupin can survive

Ten thousand years in frozen soil, it seems.
Possibly there will be at least an earth
That blossoms suddenly in snow-veined wastes.

Ten thousand years! With little chance the seed
Even of sawn-off wrens will have endured.
Let's find some solace in those legends where

Vegetables shriek. And, after all, such lack
Of men is only like one's own old age.
Besides, diviner dreams may yet be dreamed.

XVII   GOETHE'S POODLE

Goethe's pet dog, if he had one, must have grinned
During his master's talks with Eckermann;
Both so high-minded, the disciple prim.

Before the soup, a servant brings them in
A tome of topographical engravings
Or crate of tedious antiquities.

Goethe remembers Mozart as a child
But salon-pieces tinkle just ahead.
Goethe's mad science occupies their brains.

18th September, 1823:
'All my poems are occasioned poems . . .
My boy, let none say that reality

Is lacking in poetic interest.'
How much of this the younger comprehends?
How much brings sentimentally up to date?

To follow, '48. And '71.
But Eckermann by then is dead. Likewise
The putative dog, unpenned his puncturing memoirs.

Eventually Weimar stood again,
But far more sinisterly, for the deluge
Let in by classicism holed by the romantic.

As in a dream, to Eckermann appeared
That ancient, brittle, blue frock-coated legend,
Its parts composed of the Collected Works.

'Mankind is strange: as soon as a lake is frozen
Over they flock to it in hundreds, but
Who thinks how deep it is, what's in its depths?'

'True, Excellency. And the themes of *Faust*,
Right well you balanced them. And how to show
The test-tube Homunculus upon a stage?'

For what naive knowledge did that Faust give up
His soul! A fallacious theory of optics.
Quite puzzling to conceive the need to flesh

The Faustian myth when history scarcely seemed
Set on the downward path; remote, dogs roasted
Alive in millions, even devoured with relish.

XVIII   F.W. MAITLAND'S DOG

The photograph can't be assigned a date —
The one that suggests the magic of his eyes;
Liked best by Mrs M, who kept it by her.

His daughter in old age recalled the dog,
However, as a childhood friend of hers,
Her childhood of the '90s.

The dog is sitting on a table-top
Next to the eminent historian:
Its white tail trespasses upon his lap.

It, too, might well have had attractive eyes.
Both pairs have lines drawn slanting from the corner
Making the man seem as thoughtful as the dog.

XIX   MR MACMILLAN'S CAT

No marvel I'm conversing with a cat:

The curious thing is it's Macmillan's pet.
(I'm sitting by the former Premier's fire.)
It tells me its master is ignoring it.

I say: 'Why don't you jump upon his knee?
I'm sure the action wouldn't be *de trop*.'
However, the cat replies that it prefers

To wait until the guests go then come up,
From bidding them farewell, alone with Mac.
I think before I wake

How wise the cat is in the ways of love.

XX   YOUTH AND AGE

Pureness of feeling surely ought to go
With youth's inimitably shining hair.
And mostly does. Or so I must believe.

I mourn the tiny spider drowned inside
Your eye. Be careful, turning your bright head
These arachnean mornings of September.

Though empty of event, the days seem short
In middle-age. I marvel you'll have time
To play the discs that will define your past.

27

And evenings I imagined thieved by beaux
May well be given to Holmes and Monte Cristo,
Or smothering that halo with shampoo.

O years when coarseness merely made more safe
The underground ideal, how swiftly gone!
Strange the ideal should come back when we're old.

XXI THIRTY YEARS ON

I take from the shelves a book of '42
And blow the dust out of the upper edge
And open at the flyleaf quite by chance

And see my mother's love and Christmas wish
In her distinctive hand, addressed to me.
Blindingly, more than half my life comes back.

Obviously she was prompted in the choice —
The book being Francis Scarfe's on '30s poets!
Where was I then? In darkest Africa?

Her writing's vivid still because the pen
Was held between her first and second fingers.
She could be still alive, at 84.

The reason for my getting down the book
Is to see what it says of Kenneth Allott,
Just dead, born in my year of 1912.

My mother was no older when she died
Than he was, or I am. Good God, the years
Spell irony however they're cast up!

How tickled she'd have been at honours since
Acquired — the trivia of longevity
Made worthwhile for her sake.

Thinking of Allott, he by '42
Had uttered what the grudging genius
Of verse was to permit;

Though there is consolation for all those
Who loved him — as Sibelius said: 'Preserve
The themes of your youth: the best you will invent.'

I was too immature to write or care
Effectively by 1942:
The speech choked back, frustrated audience gone.

Faint memory of Christmas of that year:
A Whitmanesque night-passage through the camp;
Ratings with branches, bottles; all dead drunk.

It's certain that I never sent my thanks
So as to touch my mother's worried heart;
And now, in Allott's words, 'Too late. Too late.'

My father, before his youthful death, would find
Because of fingers-slotted pen, his bride
Of twenty-one a fascinating scribe.

Strangely, the feeling is alive today;
And his undoubted thankfulness for life,
And creativity.

XXII   THE VOYAGE

Suppose yourself alone upon a ship;
The ocean bare, the vessel under way.
Suppose a hand emerges from the deep

To grasp yours and you take it, not afraid,
But kneeling on the hard deck, welcoming
Its pull to an element inimical . . .

XXIII   CITIES AND GARDENS

Let the herbaceous border run to seed
And blow the consequent untidiness!
Eventually our birds will find the food.

One frets about the plot's economy,
The subsidies of bread and even cheese:
Suburbia surely should be self-subsisting.

Sustaining an inflated population
Mainly, it seems, of sparrows — is this right?
Here's a strange answer: they're the birds of Venus.

Tails cocked, the plumage markings point towards
The orifice of love — much patronized.
No doubt that faculty amused the goddess

And, though unlikely hauliers, won for them
The job of teaming her triumphal car.
What point have cities or their gardens if

They fail the Cyprian Queen's absurd demands?

XXIV   OVATE DREAMS

Birds dream in the egg, Professor Jouvet says.
Dreams stranger than those dreamt as, sleeping on
The wing, they change the Fall for Africa.

All's preparation for cold dwarfish days.
Who'll see them out have speckled pinafores
Or yellow sabled with a careful brush.

Dream on, in tramontana or in snow!
The exiles dream of home, the rest of song,
Of eggs and of their former ovate dreams.

Why is the soul united to the flesh?
Ancient Plotinus thrashed the matter out:
No wonder he appears in Yeats's verse.

Cold-blooded creatures, such as fish or frogs,
Don't dream, the bold professor further says.
But how's the flesh sent up the unsaline falls

And the sun prince released from clammy skin?

XXV ELEGIES

Had these been written from a castle on
The Adriatic, all (in Kai Lung's words)
Might have been 'permeated with the odour

Of joss-sticks, and honourable high-mindedness'.
As it is, I note a rain-drop either end
The garden-roller's horizontal bar.

What depth of art is this that seizes on
The peradventures of the weather for
Its inspiration materials?

— Though poets in such swarms admittedly
Could scarcely be thematically sustained
Save by the moods and flowers of temperate zones.

In fact the days were philosophical;
And then the classic sun and sky were blown
To smithereens one dusk of indigo.

But how did you expect the season's end
If not in heavenly artillery
And vulgar yellow switchings on and off?

The curious thing is that such days return —
Though mornings weepier, evenings heavier-browed;
Yet calm and warm the afternoons once more.

And the long year has still the days in store
When from the elms fall slanting showers of gold
And crisp as snow rasp at the lingering shoe,

Before the tan is muddied on the tar.
Times like the world of late antiquity
Amazingly enjoyed in its decline —

Tenth century pagan country gentlemen
Who thought that Christianity implied
The end of science; Greeks in deepest Turkey!

The lenient summer's nearly made us feel
Guests of an elegy-bewitched princess,
Hosts to enfolding unbedraggled wings.

XXVI   HEART DISEASE

Pain at my heart now, rather a relief,
Since twinges in most other parts denote
A lingering death, in my mythology.

One's sixties find the body's provinces
Needlessly dissident, for they enjoy
Already an unwilled autonomy

Disturbing to the so-called government.
Neither night's gears nor hootings bring a sense
Of reassuring common fate. Then I

Get up and see the rotten windfalls sipped
By butterflies. The dictionary says
The reason of the name's unknown — although

Early Dutch, *boterschijte*, alluded to
The baby's yellow of its excrement.
And I'm once more caught up by art and life!

Risking what Mrs Browning called its 'red
Embers' against pale blue, a specimen
Indulgently lights upon my sweatered heart.

More pain (a tender one!) to note that where
Two hinges, seemingly well-oiled, are set
To slam the enigmatic Rorschach shut

The wings themselves shade down to duskiness —
Mysterious colour of the body, furred,
Lanky and waisted as an odalisque;

Enviably palpitating only for a day.

XXVII   READING AT NIGHT
ABOUT MARCUS AURELIUS

'The gods are always there to show their power.
They help us humans in their marvellous ways:
They send us dreams; and they it is provide

The oracles for our uncertainties
And remedies for our ill-health. In fact,
They care for us and for our metropoles.'

Too *outré* even for an emperor,
Such words, we think, who've never felt at home
(Nor ever will do) in the universe.

I hope the sparrows roosting in the shrub
Above my window (presences only leaked
By droppings on the sill) sleep more than I.

They may include the hen I saw today
Pick up a small white feather in her bill
And make herself look like an elderly

Colonel, no doubt retired — as now I am.
Perhaps the sparrow did it to amuse.
Perhaps some bird-god does look after us

In such things of no consequence — though I'm
The last to under-rate the trivial
Or comic. 'Like an ill-roasted egg,' I say,

Shifting the ovoid in the simmering pan
As I prepare an early breakfast, struck
With the Swan's penchant for the homely trope.

This is the dismal week when Auden died.
He certainly was hooked up to the gods
As far as we're concerned. Though he himself —

Needing a decent drink, then off to what
More usually was maybe uncertain sleep —
I daresay felt mortal like the rest of us.

And really more than holiness, it's booze
And cigarettes make bearable our lives.
Then cut them short; and leave us to the gods.

XXVIII   ESSENTIAL MEMORY

Fourth of October 1973:
I pick the date to form a line of these
Iambics that keep falling in in threes.

Future historians, and epistolists
On cyclic weather patterns to *The Times*,
May note that I still wore a summer suit.

The bloody oblong that the creeper seems
Beyond the lavatory's striated pane
Astonishes the calls of nature still.

Its life, however, must be told in days.
And even Auden, unforgettable
Because of his creativeness, begins

To fade as what he was: the body — loved,
Or awesome but indifferent natural object —
Breaks up beneath the top-soil of Kirschstetten.

The tractor crawls along — is making! — that
Curved difference between the green and brown
Upon the tilted upland. Here is what

Essential memory depends upon.
For if the plough should fail, the superstructure
Collapses. Howard Newby tells me that

The night of Auden's death he was himself
In Vienna, near that fatal-roomed hotel,
Not knowing Auden there, still less his end.

As what he was. In spite of Howard's health,
Comparative youth, quite soon none will recall
What Auden's 'world' was like when first created.

Autumn: the leaf more insecurely hangs
Than hung the fruit. Nights longer. Weather worse.
Noise of the rain brings other noises near.

Can we love retrospectively the dead
We never really knew? I start to think so;
Especially since there is no question of

Unwished for or unrequited love. And now
The blood's all trickled to the ground; the voice
Only on tape; speculatively warm the clasp.

XXIX   JOWETT'S NOTEBOOK

Benjamin Jowett's notebook thoughts strike home:
A man of sixty should collect the young
About him, and lead quiet *al fresco* days . . .

'My life has been a waste of vanity
And egoism.' And:
'I ought to rid myself of shyness which

Has detracted from my life at least a third.'
While reading his biography in bed
I rise to get an apple from the shed

And find myself at five
Under skies mythical, euclidean . . .
The Master's gospel of hard, unselfish work,

How much it now appeals — alas, too late!
How curious that today
The virtuous has become unfashionable!

Autumn takes hold. A garden chair must be
Conveyed to eccentric sites to catch the sun,
Which indoors fingers long-neglected books.

Those greying heavens just before the dawn
More or less feebly lit with yellow points:
Diagrams of tremendous destiny

I was too nervous ever to embrace!

XXX   LATE OCTOBER

As crossly as a child
I stared out at the rain.
Then summer came again.

The miracle, however,
Was one of resurrection
In death-bed frailty.

The sunlight warm enough
To live in gay as beasts
Must now be told in hours —

Although this wasp seems quite
Nonchalant, washing its face,
Anchored on four still legs.

XXXI   SOLDIER'S MOON

So, you are shining still, as bright at two
As evening. Now you print the window's bar
On my abandoned page, when earlier

You chalked the city roofs' alternate slopes.
How long and patiently you shine for night's
Infrequent wayfarers!

Your orb reminds me of the bladder's shape
On x-ray negatives — as firm and white.
Strange reassurance of good health down there.

But do I really want to live into
A world of hook-nosed Arab fighting Jew,
The puny sides sustained by evil States?

Still later, heating milk, I see you cast
Darkness the other way — the chimney's shaft
On the pale eastern wall.

My nights are as disturbed as soldiers' are:
Perhaps as dangerous! Our little lives
Are bad enough without the man-made risk.

Dead world, shine on! What interrupts your glare
Can only be of fleeting consequence:
Scorpions and rocks, tall miles of precious air.

XXXII   THE VERDICT

The verdict has already been arrived
At. But the foreman of the jury still
Must write the record down laboriously;

And others of the panel go and pee
Or phone to say they will be home for tea,
Before all shamble back into the Court

And the judge summoned from his crossword puzzle.
So that some time goes by before his fate
Can possibly be learnt by the accused.

And more: this was arrived at earlier still —
Before the charge was laid, the jury called,
The trial started. To the prisoner

It comes as no surprise to find himself
Condemned to death. The circumstances merely
(Though often attempted to be conjured up)

Strike him as somewhat odd or poignant. Who
Could have foretold that he would be cut off
During a visit from his fleeting Muse;

Or that he'd be less anguished than embarrassed;
Feel more for his survivors than himself;
Making some verses out of hopeless dread

Of rather more than average tedium?

XXXIII   DEATH OF HENRY JAMES

I read while walking (*à la* Gide) beneath
Continuously leaf-releasing trees.
It's the well-known but always gripping tale

Of James struck down upon the bedroom floor.
'So here it is at last, the distinguished thing.'
Genius in threatened death as in his art:

Discrimination, interest and *sang-froid*
Instead of lesser talents' vulgar dread.
Dread at not being stoical enough,

At proving not to have worked hard enough,
Simply at not being good enough, when faced
With the unpleasant parting from one's works.

Why does one skate so near oblivion's hole?
Of course, the poetry it wants to write
Flows rarely from the third or fourth rate nib.

This metre almost that of *Feversham*,
Oozing with *River Duddon* sentiments:
An awkward play, a sequence of decline —

Although not quite desired and in a sense
Unwilled, the words must by and large be right;
For other words belong to better men.

Fourth of November: wasps still crawling on
The ivy flowers, mere withered spheres. And yet
The skies are huge from half-gone foliage.

'Farewell, the latter spring!
Farewell, All Hallown summer!' Not for long,
Surely, can winter's couriers be delayed.

But James got well. His actual death, though made
Bizarre with Bonapartist fantasies,
Perhaps was liker to our conjectured own.

Quaffing the frightful draught, named in *Macbeth*,
Precursor to the following day's x-rays,
I dimly sense the distinguished heritage —

And suck the lingering sweetness from the globe.

XXXIV   MEMORIES OF WAR

Tonight dreams may be had
(To take an instance of my own conceits)
About the one-legged dancers of the Chad.

39

But now the unromantic dominates.
From the long ward beyond my little room
Come uninhibited sounds, among them groans.

As well as farting, men could be dying there.
The feeling of a war-time mess returns
So strongly as to occasion more alarm

Than that tomorrow's probing will reveal
Malignancy implanted deep within.
Even the music in the ear-phones tritely

Augments the sense of thirty years ago.
Dear comrades, now we well may have to die,
Our span being up or proximately up.

But youth can be kept from the conscripted ranks
That trail the alleyways between the beds
And lie awake or half-asleep on beds

At doom's grossly lessened odds.

XXXV   THE OTHER SIDE

'You've had your operation, Mrs Brown.
Wake up!' The cry undoubtedly recurs
(It seems to me, who's also lying there,

Scarcely more wide awake than Mrs Brown)
In some congested docking-station for
The dead. The utter strangers strewn about,

The sexes intermingled sexlessly;
The far-off burning of an ancient pain
In my prone, sheeted figure; busy, white

Androgynous attendants; and the lack
Of memory of things before, confirm
After-life's ludicrous reality.

XXXVI   POST-OPERATIVE

Since one's dead drunk or, rather,
Just through dead drunkenness —
Not yet hung over, though —

One wonders why the fun
Of getting drunk somehow
Has skipped the memory.

I expound this to a sprite
In perfect white, but she
Ignores the snail's slurred speech.

Later, I see I never
Made clear I really knew
I was sloshed on pentathol.

Such missing links in their chain
Of discourse is what makes
Drunks so terribly boring.

For them existence tends
To the incorporeal —
Cherubim, proneness, quibble.

XXXVII   *HEILIGE DANKGESANG*

Sunset: the balding tree
Filters a sudden flight of darkling birds,
Seeming to gain a leaf or two thereby.

Why don't I, lying here,
Give joyous thanks my life is still preserved?
Perhaps I do so, in my grudging way.

Succeeding salmon clouds,
Untidy smoky clouds come swiftly on,
As though cranked by the deviser of a masque.

41

The unlikely blue of sky
Fades soon, as well it might. But isn't there
Even more virtue in the commonplace?

If one can call it such:
Baroque but normal flutings of the pipes;
Thorndyke, the doctor on the bedside chair;

The aircraft, winking now
Across the gold half-moon, about to drop
Merely a load unseasonably tanned.

XXXVIII   A STRANGE DEVICE

I see an advert for the Spatter Guard —
Device for keeping fat confined when frying.
Though we already own two Spatter Guards

I tear the coupon from the newspaper,
Thinking I ought to guard against the day
When we might be without a Spatter Guard.

Rather presuming on longevity —
Possession of three sturdy Spatter Guards;
And that digestion will not even falter

In modest toleration of the fried.
But let us order one more Spatter Guard
(Or even two) and demonstrate our faith.

Moreover, does it matter at the close
That we have unused ingenuity
To leave our heirs — who may not know that grease

Is kept from elsewhere by the Spatter Guard,
Or that it shields mankind from boiling oil,
Or of its emblematic qualities?

XXXIX   THE WINDOW-CLEANERS

Today was overheard
Our old censorious window-cleaner say
'The garden is the proper place for birds.'

Terrace and even sills
Are on their way to being as wholly iced
As some mid-ocean-beaten, igneous perch.

No wonder that he feels
Constrained to excuse the milieu to his mate,
Newly acquired, unused to a poet's panes.

Good job he doesn't come
Inside the house, where moralists might trace
The evidence of parson's noses still.

Yes, lured by kindness, birds
In summer ventured here and then took fright:
Innocent Choctaws brought to the *faubourgs*.

Too easy synonym,
'Kindness', for stale soaked bread and pity spent
On lives at present sterner than our own . . .

We hop quite boldly in
Then panic at the strangeness caging us,
Find windows only feigning liberty.

Our aim is for the soul
To enter on the earth and be sustained;
Then without hindrance whirr into the skies.

Ambiguous the role
That such as window-cleaners play: deceit
With crystal but dissevering barricades.

XL   STILL AT LARGE

I could be so immersed, like Gibbon, 'in
The passage of the Goths over the Danube'
As to miss dinner time.

The difference is he wouldn't have envisaged
Barbarians as threatening his age
Or coming from his set.

And similarly when old Jowett said
That medieval folk were like ourselves
But 'dirtier in their habits'

He'd not in mind the return of maniacs
As heads of state or even torturers
As minor civil servants.

So how have I been able all through life
To write and utter rather more than less
Of what I wanted to?

By helping philistines control the land;
By getting nothing for my work in art;
By squandering priceless time.

To let me stay at large is their award
For service; or the evidence, more like,
Of my art's impotence.

XLI   NOTES ON ART

For Huw Wheldon

O 'green-eyed dumplings with an astral stare' —
Thus Schoenberg's paintings, rather well described.
Those who've contrived to cover up in art

Their turgid rhetoric or romantic souls
Should keep from practising another art,
Where dim technique may give the game away.

Now Wilfrid Mellers admitted when he heard
The Elgar symphony of 1910
After 'experimental' works, it made

The events of sixty years astonishing —
The melancholy and heroic changed
To mutterings that dehumanize; and yet

Still didn't call the latter green-eyed balls.
Critics make each successive *Zeitgeist* more
Patently turnip-headed than before.

Surely I've bored the world with this already,
Just as I must have more than once observed
That every pigeon wears pale riding-breeches.

Even technique can't hide that art's about
What moves non-artists. TV (as you said)
Is telling stories, like George Eliot.

Astute of Anthony Powell to extirpate
The story-teller's soft interior,
Not least to leave more room for irony.

The astral stare: yes, that we must admit
(For who denies the rumminess of life?)
But flashed from Mrs Erdleigh, not the hero.

If the poetic vision is considered —
Sharper perception, most things slotting in,
Amused affection, even for ugliness —

Isn't the poem's importance obvious,
Since this is just what all would wish to feel?
Unless reared on a diet of mad dumplings.

XLII FATHERS

My father may be often in my dreams
Yet (since he died when I was young) play parts —
Or be himself — and stay unrecognized.

In any case dreaming often modifies
The features of the characters we know,
Though usually telling us who's really meant,

Like useful footnotes to an allegory.
This morning speckled foam fell in the basin:
Watching my father shave came flooding back

From over fifty years. His cut-throat razor,
Black beard, seemed things of fascinated love —
And now replace the visage and his speech.

Did he imagine (as I sometimes do)
His son would one day reach the age of sixty,
Himself being almost *ipso facto* dead?

Worse, in his final illness did he think
How he would leave a foolish child of eight,
Himself being hardly out of folly's years?

XLIII LATE NOVEMBER

Even at two light's slow decline begins:
Hardly worth starting more affairs of day.
Let's doze, then drink some tea and watch the clouds . . .

Moon in the west sky, ready to be gilt:
Just time before the scotch and poetry
To go and get my shoes — soled, quarter-heeled.

A lady with a pug-dog on a lead
Is saying at the counter how he's been
Attacked by un-led dogs upon his way.

I ask her why I haven't seen of late
The dog at large in our secluded lane.
Reply: 'I never let him off the lead.'

It turns out there's a *doppelgänger* pug.
Do all pugs look alike? It may be so.
Perhaps the freely wandering pug is dead.

Yes, the route home's illumined by the bright
Sliver of moon. The frosty air compels
Breathing as noisy as the squash-nosed pug's.

The curtains drawn, loudspeakers speaking Kern,
I start to wonder what should body out
Astounding images and silvery words —

Canine personae, moon-glow, comic life?

XLIV   CULTURAL HISTORY

The suburb's life: I've only to go out
To find it subtly changing, like a sky.
The little grocer's now sells 'Pork Farms' pies.

Gombrich maintains that it's an elusive thing,
The mentality of people in a street;
Can't be retrieved or even be described.

Eight p, a patron of the baker's shop
Argues is still the price of sandwich loaves,
What she's been asked for at her usual branch.

'The small tin's eight, the sandwich loaf is nine' —
The assistant's borne out by a printed list;
Advises adherence to the other branch!

The almost metaphysical dispute
Obscures what was behind the original point:
Nine new pence for a stunted staff of life.

Or one-and-nine in ancient cash. I see
The note-book given me some years ago
By Georg Rapp cost only two-and-two

And still serves to record my night-time thoughts —
Which share, as may be seen, the fugitive
Preoccupations of suburbanites.

Nice if they knew the rest of my concerns:
But possibly their children will come round
To Marx's theory of the price of bread

And all myth's golden emblems for the grain.

XLV   END OF THE CHEAP FOOD ERA

I check my meagre purchases to see
How the enormous total has been reached.
The culprit is a pound of sausages.

Admittedly, they're Marks and Spencer's best,
Said to be 'over 90% pure pork':
Still, they're a somewhat novel luxury.

We always vowed the revolution would
Arrive when life became intolerable —
Which term we might well have envisaged as

The prospect of not affording sausages.

XLVI   THE APPROACH OF THE COMET

A human of androgynous *tournure*
Opens the shutter of 'The Topless Bar',
A bookshop on the fringes of Soho.

Kohoutek draws inexorably near.
One's been on the look out for the death of kings
And for the first glimpse of the hairy star.

When did it visit us before? Perhaps
Prehistory saw it under bony brows;
Or farther back its long ellipse corralled

An earth as loose and formless as itself —
Refrigerated nothingness and dust.
Pre-dawns of sleeplessness, I rise and hurry

To the paved garden, shivering in my gown,
And scan with binoculars
The offered range of light: from yellow lamps

In newly-naked boughs along the lane
To the gigantic hunter's outlined frame.
What do I so absorbedly search for? Doom?

I found, some weeks ago, through illness, that
I should be far from glad to say farewell —
Denying a lifetime's pessimistic vein.

I visualise the possibility
Of non-doom, which almost jealously I see
You may enjoy, darling posterity.

So far the comet fails to catch my eye.
The monarch seems to be in perfect health.
The shutter rattles up 'The Topless Bar'.

XLVII   WAITING FOR THE BARBARIANS

The pay-off of Cavafy's famous poem:
The let-down that the vandals never came.
My modest *aperçu* is that they're here.

Like androids, or beings from another world,
They take the shape of ordinary men,
Even the Jones or Robinson we know.

Then when they form a huge majority
They will reveal their ghastly taste, their lust
For violence, and indifference to death.

What am I thinking? 'Will reveal'? All bosh.
Impatient with slow progress here and there,
Most have declared themselves and taken over.

Too late to sway the president with art;
Mere plastic pumps, the hearts that might be moved;
The brain a convoluted programmed tape.

'I celebrate the instinct's primacy.
To cast my verses into metric shape
Would be betrayal of their heaven-sent form.'

Thus the one voice of multiplying bards
Who claim to be inheritors of the past
Though hairy, barefoot, clad in smelly skins.

XLVIII   STRANGE MEETING

In Boots the Chemists an oldish fellow bars my way —
An eye to eye encounter as I try to pass
Into another part of the emporium.

He wears a sober navy overcoat. His hair's
Indubitably salt and pepper. His regard
Is one of semi-recognition, tinged with alarm.

As may already have been guessed, I've misconceived
A mirrored wall as a communicating door.
I turn with a muttered oath: the old boy disappears.

The young boy still continues on his foolish course.

XLIX   GUILTY

I know that some must surely think of me
As of potential criminality.
I grin at children, actually converse

With lolling babes in prams by banks and shops
And go along the supermarket shelves
Without the prescribed receptacle of wire.

Also, already I've an old man's laugh:
I wonder how soon the speaking voice will follow —
Sounding like some droll actor playing Shallow.

When they arrest me I'll have no defence.
Useless to say I wanted to express
My solidarity with those who grapple

With tricycles and pups; or sympathize
With tears at neglect, wet nappies and the cold;
Or put the butter where it shouldn't go

Quite inadvertently. 'You planned to make
Contact with little boys and, more so, girls.
You'd have ripped infants from their mothers' care.'

The quavering plea of guilty comes. But wait
A bit. For this I always meant to pay.
There's nothing Freudian in theft. Oh yeah?

Again, a bird-lover stroking cats for pity?
Clearly the man's a member of the gang
That goes round nicking moggies for their fur.

Named in the *South East London Mercury*,
It may be for the surreptitious stowing
Of beans, or Persians with pavement-sweeping hair;

Certainly not for fame in poetry.

No wonder society is in a mess.
The trousers tweedy, very wide, with cuffs;
The shoes have soles four inches thick and tops

Brown plastic, trimmed with lemon. What on earth
Provokes man to discomfort and grotesque
Appearance (I say nothing of his mug)?

No wonder the individual's in a mess.
Terrible forces work to ruin taste —
Unless the ruination is innate.

And as to that, I see a survey showed
That classical music positively hurt
The tenants on some working-class estate.

All tends to make reactionary chumps
As well as fashionably comic youth.
Is no one to be taken seriously?

Three planets shining in the southern sky
Before star-shine (unusual, I should think)
Prove winter may be enjoyed not merely borne.

Should one ignore boneheaded fashion's rule,
The oil sheiks buying guns, the philistines
Training as fodder for the demagogues,

Content that this temporary observation-post,
Even when burnt-out as its satellite
(Now climbing to outshine its fellow discs)

Will rise with others in December skies?
It was when winter first was loved by man
He saw the patterns of a frosty night

Made scientific sense not destiny.
Brief epoch: following his nakedness;
Before voluminous pants and shitty shoes.

LI FROM THE JOKE SHOP

'Why doesn't somebody buy *me* false ears?'
I can't help remarking as I pack the same,
Plus a few boils and scars, in Christmas paper.

Returning from a stroll some hours later,
I see my ears are big and red enough.
Even a scar may be discerned. Life-long

Ambition to amuse fulfilled, it seems,
Without adventitious aid. Although some boils,
God-given, might more surely make for laughs.

LII WATCHING TV

I brush my tickling cheeks and find them wet.
How silly to sit here alone and weep;
Moreover, at vicarious events.

And yet I recognize the attitude
As demonstrating the essential man —
Only required is, after switching off,

To dance before my wife like Jack Buchanan,
Breathing a song of seaside infancy;
Or warble Tosti in the lavatory:

Attention to the tears diverted thus.
What curious masks I've worn all through my life!
And yet how can I call them masks that hid

From time to time in private that fair face
Of reason, not to mention compromise?
There's been one mask and several characters.

I thought for forty years the bourgeoisie
When it took arms would have to be fought back.
And now with Lewis, Owen and Sassoon

(And hairy purchasers of stone-ground flour)
Perhaps what I believe is that it's wrong
In any circumstance to take a life.

Not that the bourgeoisie has changed its spots,
As proved once more by Chile's recent times,
Yet here's a foolish Cambridge English don

Imputing in *Encounter* magazine
Pardon or love of violence in the '30s
To the intelligentsia of the left.

As though it wasn't war they tried to scotch,
As though they gained by moving from their class,
As though the age allowed mild remedies.

No doubt our academic might conjoin
This view with sniffling in one's sixties at
Schoolmasters refereeing football games.

But since I'm part of what's to be replaced
I give away the secret of my rheum
And of my comic or ironic turns;

For surely in the new society
Such matters must survive — and grow. That's why
We bothered with those selfless chores of youth.

LIII   DEBUSSY, WALTON, KYUNG-WHA CHUNG

Why don't I play the record more of these
Douze études by Debussy, since their beauty
Differs so little from titles less austere?

Why don't I stand and see the sunset out
More nights than this? Admittedly, the trees
And chimneys coal a sky of fiercest fire

That makes one think December's turning point
More than theoretical. Why don't I haunt
Museums of fine art and schools for girls?

Man can bear only so much pulchritude.
Upon another record-sleeve I see,
With quite offhand benevolence, the old

Composer clasping a fiddler in his arms.

LIV   WINTER SOLSTICE

December's early-ending but forbearant days
Produce long bands of bird-egg blue or primrose skies
Divided by angry greys

That threaten to annex the total heavens — though
Rather surprisingly time's left for birds to fly
And even in a tree

Linger and if they're blackbirds play their xylophones.
Premature duskiness makes sparrows sharp as wrens.
Then when the day looks gone

The robin's rattle sounds from seeming birdless boughs.
What am I doing in this world of Georgian verse,
That carries sanguine news?

LV   LOVE

> *Give me back my life.*
> *Come back to Sorrento.*

What words! Dare hardly use them, even for
An epigraph. They wring me like the tale
By Chekhov, 'The Lady With the Little Dog'.

— Poignant enough before the Heifits film
Transformed it into silvery images,
Backed by an unknown's harrowing melody.

Oh yes, it's true that lives can be carved up
By forfeiting the only one they love.
The contrary appears not to apply:

Having achieved content, we seek in vain
In Yalta or elsewhere the bliss of how
It was in the beginning. As in youth.

LVI   RHETORIC AND MELODY

Christmas away: returning find *Bleak House*
Unshifted from my bedside chair. What's more,
Still lurking in familiar haunts, the Muse —

The Jamesian benediction part somehow
Conferred on, part self-generated by
Ageing creators; which they're coy about

Since if she goes their lives will lack all point.
And what have they to offer her to stay?
Strolling round my estate, I see through nude

Branches the pallid moon of afternoon
Now shrunken to a bracket. Days stretch out
Of trying to boil existence down to words.

The Boodles and the Buffys still hold power;
The cog-wheels of society don't engage;
The Dedlocks well could last in Lincolnshire.

One has to come back home to gauge the size
And possibly the nature of one's love —
Although I see quite clearly that my life's

Been pauperized by a shyness to confess.
For hardly recompense to show in art
The things one should have influenced in fact.

Dear child, who lives unknowingly those last
Few months or even weeks of childhood, what
Embrace or reassurance could I give?

I play my Christmas-present records, green
With envy at Ravel's command of tart
Rhetoric and memorable melody.

The play of *Cinderella* that we saw
Confirms above all else the everyday
Lust for the triumph of the beautiful —

Though you'll find adulthood is otherwise.
'What the poor are to the poor is little known . . . '
'A certain Jarndyce in an evil hour . . . '

But who would wish to multiply the moon;
Change the well-tempered scale (and yet they do)?
I hope the slipper fits. I know it will.

LVII   *AGES IN THE MAKING*

To W.M. Balch

I'm glad you sent a copy of this work —
A history of Great and Little Waltham.
Over the years you've almost made me, too,

An Essex man! The gift arrived in days
Of strikes, go-slows, and strictured Arab oil:
Some are prognosticating England's doom.

I leaf the photographic section over:
Here, the almshouses at Scrapfaggots Green;
The girls at the Girls' School all in pinafores;

The Boys' School as it was in 1900
('Several boys . . . later killed in World War I');
Ladies (with hats) cocking barley in that war;

George Marshall carting mangel-worzels; Fred
Johnson, corn-dolly maker; and the sun-burnt
Founders of the Waltham WI;

The band on Pleasant Sunday Afternoons —
Strings, clarinet and what seems penny whistle.
And is the legacy of this to end?

Have we let down these men of numerous skills,
Respectable women, knickerbockered boys
Who leap-frogged in the carless village street;

And farther back in time — the Iron Age
And Domesday Walthamers, who must have felt,
Like sparrows, their generations guaranteed?

As I grow crustier, ideology
Seems less and less to matter. One hangs on
To judging whether colleagues would stand up

Against the intrusion of a Roman nose,
A sovereign who thought himself too too divine,
Or anyone who tried to twist the law.

Perhaps I always was a patriot;
Or predisposed, at any rate, to craft,
Hard work, jaw-breaking Anglo-Saxon names,

An island life, anachronistic, taciturn!

LVIII   EXCHANGE OF NEWS

For Jabez

Mysterious cobalt droppings in North Wales!
It seems mice ate a *papier-mâché* bowl
During your absence since the summer days.

We've no news so spectacular in exchange.
Our substitute for nature, Greenwich Park
('Not equal,' Boswell said, 'to Fleet Street'), strewn

Derangedly through its vistas though it is,
After the gales, with antlers from great trees,
Can't match your rodents, patriots and steeps.

Obsessions of romanticism: falls
And fanfares. You may have the former; we
Just hear the young Saint-Saëns on radio.

The Gallic sensibility in art
That even saved Saint-Saëns in his excesses
(But not precluding pathos) we both admire;

And yet it comes that all unconsciously
I've taken as the model for this work
The *Night Thoughts* of the pompous Edward Young.

The stiff iambics and insomnia,
The moralising tone — the very same.
Thank God (thank God!) I'm not devout as well.

You tell me what I know I ought to do —
More of the anecdotal; but not much
Happens to ruminants like the Reverend Young . . .

Travis and Emery's shop in Cecil Court:
I riffle through the music stacked outside.
I think I shan't be buying *How To Master*

The Tenor Banjo. Curious, writing this,
I momentarily can't place the ictus on
'Banjo' and have to get the dictionary.

All the more strange when later I recall
My long ago unfinished — hardly started —
Verse on a paradigm of Wittgenstein's:

'Asked to select a banjo from some things,
He merely picked an instrument with strings.'
The word proves to be a corruption of 'bandore',

A kind of lute the Elizabethans knew;
As 'What's her haire? faith two Bandora wiars.'
Unlikely story on the face of it —

Resembling, somewhat, mouse shit of bright blue.

LIX   VARIATION ON CAVAFY

You will not meet the Laestrygonians,
The Cyclops, furious Poseidon (wrote
Cavafy) unless you have them in your soul.

I wish that I myself could be so sure
Either of coming history or my soul.
Where are the huge Sicilian cannibals —

In healing art or in reality?
Who knows if horror of the smothering god
Isn't one's own suppressed desire to kill?

Burn the ghost apples of the previous summer,
The gardening notes command. Already shoots
Appear under naked trees. What presences

Shall we require to exorcise next year?

LX   THE FUTURE

It's early February. Snowdrops crowd
As close and with as coy dropped heads as some
Green-leotarded, white-capped *corps de ballet*.

Dusk; and a robin sings in actual moonlight.
Ambiguous time; my birthday time. One year,
A frozen waste; another, song and dance.

Rhubarb's sore fingers peep already after
'The mildest January since '32' —
Year of my twentieth; month, no doubt (I don't

Recall!), of bonus kisses out of doors.
What wretched verse I surely then produced
(All luckily destroyed or in a trunk).

But then I apply the epithet to that
Produced in '42, *et caetera.*
I come indoors and play my latest discs.

There seems to be a basic mode of art
To aim for in this troubled epoch yet,
As well as did the eight-years-old Mozart:

Below a melody *cantabile,*
A busy figuration; what the sleeve-
Note calls the *singenden Allegro-stil.*

However, useless envying those who wrote
In more auspicious periods for taste —
No part of artistry is automatic;

Artists' self-betterment the least of all.
This other sleeve-note's wet but right: Poulenc
'Listened to the little song he had within.'

A third pronounces that 'The *guzlas* dream
As they accompany the serenades' —
Phrase from an unknown Wallace Stevens poem!

Better than I, birds sense the future's here
And even in the sudden creamy snow,
Cow-clapped next morning from a false-ceilinged sky

(Making the ballet's *décor* Muscovite),
Still swear to take the decades on and on.
Somehow they hear the *guzlas* dream: as ever,

Their love *alfresco* and their singing spry.

LXI   TWENTY YEARS OF
THE POETRY BOOK SOCIETY

New Zealand House, Haymarket. Sixteenth floor.
The city's white and greys and sudden green
Fill all the vista to the arching blue.

Cruelly level at this chopper's height,
The February sun. It shines on poets
Invited for an anniversary drink

And makes the party like the last in Proust.
To see bent veins, thin hair, large corporations,
Almost cheers one about one's own decay.

Dear co-slaves of the Muse, I might, if pressed
(The mid-day boozing clearly starts to work),
Approve your various poetries *en bloc.*

Such funny shapes to seek the beautiful,
Such feeble minds to make a cogent form,
Such egotists to interpret life and nature!

Are all we present mutual friends — or foes?
And does the rest of England, in the end,
Not require beauty, shape or explication?

Doubtless some fellow poets eyeing my
Trousers of daring check, plus clipped moustache
(With other curious traits that I don't see),

Are thereby confirmed in their low estimate
Of what I write — being less full of scotch
And sentiment and years than now I am.

I can't help thinking how in each crazed head
This narrow craftsmen's world is broadened out —
Beyond the urban concrete to the fields;

Into the empyrean; and the past.

LXII   BEING

The dead of night. Strange sound. Unknown
Its origin. Perhaps it's in my head —
Some tumour starting to batten on my brain,

The hissing inviolate and continuous.
The February moon is full and almost
Bright enough, it seems, for me to tell

The colours so far showing round the lawn:
The six-rayed open yellow crocus suns;
Quite blue emerging leaves of daffodils.

The latter's gold I'll hope also to see,
Noise from the growth inside my cranium
Being assigned now to a fizzing gram

(See-sawing in my bedside tumbler) of
Ascorbic acid, prophylactic for
The winter's microbes (soon to disappear).

Pauling's authority in science made
Respectable this surely occult faith,
And so converted me a second time!

The hypochondriac will war against
The common cold but has to leave his guard
Wide open to the wrongly-turning cell.

Non-being wasn't in the least unpleasant:
Why should we worry at returning there?
Clearly because of this magnesium moon;

Flowers lancing through what's sepia and rotten;
Affection and respect. O months just past
Of lenient nature, ruthless human loss!

Our years arrive and go, not all forgotten.

LXIII AFTER

Some slightly swollen daffodil leaves bend over,
Choosing to flower; though days go by before
The part turned down suggests a citrine trumpet.

Wings, throats, vibrate against the murrey sky:
What bird that cataclysm destines for
My bungled care arranges to be laid?

Tea by the barely-budded almond shows
How ludicrously lenient the season.
An actual bee drinks from the man-hole cover.

If lesser natural orders undertake
To see things through, then surely so must I;
Maybe in worsening times and certainly

In worsening shape. It seems to me that after
Sixty-two Springs I'm still an amateur
Not just of gardens and wild birds but of

Lived history as well. For don't I see
The coming revolution needed merely
To usher in a rather safer life?

For families in hives, of shoots, of starlings, too.